Aberdeenshire
COUNCIL

Aberdeenshire Libraries
www.aberdeenshire.gov.uk/libraries
Renewals Hotline 01224 661511

HOOPMAN.
INSIDE ASPERGONGOS.

Inside Asperger's
Looking Out

KATHY HOOPMANN

Jessica Kingsley *Publishers*
London and Philadelphia

First published in 2013
by Jessica Kingsley Publishers
116 Pentonville Road
London N1 9JB, UK
and
400 Market Street, Suite 400
Philadelphia, PA 19106, USA

www.jkp.com

Copyright © Kathy Hoopmann 2013
All photographs courtesy of Shutterstock.co.uk

Front cover image source: Shutterstock®.

Library of Congress Cataloging in Publication Data
A CIP catalog record for this book is available from the Library of Congress

British Library Cataloguing in Publication Data
A CIP catalogue record for this book is available from the British Library

ISBN 978 1 84905 334 1
eISBN 978 0 85700 670 7

Printed and bound in China
by Broad Link Enterprise Ltd

For my unique friends,

Judit Kiss and

Abigail Guinevere Joy Schoorl Kiss

also by Kathy Hoopmann

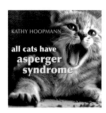

**All Cats Have
Asperger Syndrome**
ISBN 978 1 84310 481 0

All Dogs Have ADHD
ISBN 978 1 84310 651 7
eISBN 978 1 84642 840 1

Asperger Adventures

Blue Bottle Mystery
An Asperger Adventure
ISBN 978 1 85302 978 3
eISBN 978 1 84642 169 3

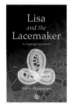

Lisa and the Lacemaker
An Asperger Adventure
ISBN 978 1 84310 071 3
eISBN 978 1 84642 354 3

Of Mice and Aliens
An Asperger Adventure
ISBN 978 1 84310 007 2
eISBN 978 0 85700 179 5

Haze
ISBN 978 1 84310 072 0
eISBN 978 1 84642 405 2

A Note from the Author

I am enormously indebted to Tony and Sarah Attwood, Wendy Lawson, John Elder Robison, Janet Eiby, Pauline Thomas, Peggy and Jadd Lawand, Judit Kiss and Abigail Guinevere Joy Schoorl Kiss, Kay Bridges, Janette and Robert Meulen, Marie and David Oldfield (my ever-loving parents), and Karl, Shani and Becky (my amazing kids) for reading the early drafts and giving invaluable feedback. Thank you also to the parent group at AEIOU Autism Centre for your helpful comments. And finally to my wonderful husband, Errol, thank you for giving me the time and space to write and for not making me earthbound.

Kathy Hoopmann

In general, a person with Asperger syndrome, or high-functioning autism, is someone who may have:

- ◦ difficulties relating to others in social situations
- ◦ difficulties understanding nonverbal communication
- ◦ heightened sensitivity to touch, sight, hearing, taste and smell
- ◦ set routines and a strong preference for order
- ◦ an intense ability to focus in specific interest areas
- ◦ great loyalty towards others
- ◦ a unique mind which is able to see life from a new perspective.

But as you read, remember that not every person with Asperger syndrome, or Aspies as they are fondly known, must have all the traits mentioned in this book, and they may have some that are not mentioned. Two Aspies can be extreme opposites in personality and behaviour and still both be Aspies. By understanding their strengths and weaknesses and providing encouragement and support, you can help Aspies to flourish and reach their full and wonderful potential.

OK, let's get a few things settled right from the start.

People with Asperger syndrome are not broken,
or damaged, or somehow less than 'normal' people.
We do not need to be 'fixed', and we don't 'suffer'
from Asperger's as if it is a disease.

Sure, we may think and act and learn
differently from others,

but different can be a good thing.

Even those with Asperger syndrome can be very different from each other.

We can be shy or outgoing, depressed or happy, be alone or have friends, struggle or excel, be fussy or eat anything.

There are, however, a few things that we do have in common.

Consider our senses. They can be hyper alert. Got that? HYPER. It's as though our senses input button is turned right up.

Some foods, which
others think are yummy
and healthy, can taste

Yuck!

to us.

We are not trying
to be difficult.

We'd like to eat what others eat,
 but sometimes it feels slimy or bad
 or just plain *wrong*.

If we say that a sound annoys us, we really mean it.

Even the scratching of pencil on paper
   or the buzz of a light can drill into our ears
      until we will do anything to shut the noise out.

But sounds that
we control or make
ourselves do not
bother us at all.

Go figure, huh!

Our sense of smell can be so strong that
during everyday activities such as art class...

we can't focus because of the fumes.

Bright and flickering lights can make us feel sick
and give us headaches,

and even colours can affect us
and may swirl around
and hurt our eyes.

As for touch, why,
oh why, are we made
to wear things that
strangle and scratch?

It doesn't seem fair
that we have to be
uncomfortable all
day just to make
others happy.

When we go out, we hear noises, and we smell things,
and lights flash in our heads,

and our brains

go nuts.

When it all becomes too much,
   we may rock or flap or jump
      to make us feel like we are in control.

Some people don't like it when we do that,
and may tell us to...

But *you* try dealing with ordinary things
that scratch and smell and taste bad
and hurt your eyes and ears, and see what you would do.

Sometimes, when things get so bad, and we can't explain how we feel, and we have no idea how to control our situation, we may yell and scream and throw our bodies around.

This is called a meltdown.

Meltdowns are not fun. We can't control them.
We never choose to have one,
and hate them when they happen to us.

Often we get punished for having one,
which is so unfair as, believe us,
the meltdowns are punishment enough.

Another thing we have trouble with
                      is understanding social rules.

Even when we try hard to fit in with the crowd,

we tend to make a mess of things.

For a start, we don't know the difference between someone smiling and someone wanting to hurt us. When we meet new people, we cannot tell by how they look or how they talk if they are friendly or dangerous.

You try being
relaxed and happy
when you can't tell
anger from a yawn.

It's like this.

We don't understand body language.

We can't pick up people's feelings by the tone of their voice.

We understand the basic meanings of words.

So, when other people see, hear, and react to this...

we see, hear and
react to this,

come here
and say that!

which can get us into all sorts of trouble,
and usually we have no idea why.

When most people enter a public place,
the crowds and busyness do not bother them.

But for us, they are confusing places full of threats.

Every sense is on alert, all the time,
looking for danger,

not really
being sure

if we should be
afraid or not.

Do you have any idea how much effort that takes?

It makes us want to curl up in a ball
and be left alone.

However, we don't want to be alone all the time.

We want friends.

We really do.

But we don't know how to get them,

which is a shame because we know we are
loyal and interesting and fun to be with,
if only we are given a chance.

We've got a clever
and quirky sense
of humour.

Our skills are
really worthwhile,
like the abilities
to concentrate
on things that
interest us,

and to come up with new ideas.

We try to make friends by being helpful,
and letting people know how to do things
the right way.

And we try to explain how wonderful
it is to do the same things
in the same way every day.

7:00 am - wake

7:02 am - eat

7:05 am - explore

For some
reason, others
do not always
agree with us.

We always tell the truth.

That doesn't seem to make us popular either.

So we use logic,
      which often fails us too.

We try to make friends by sharing exciting facts about things that interest us.

And we tell others as soon as we see them
because we do not know how long they will stay
and we do not want them to miss out.
But often they get bored, or walk away,
or tell us to stop going on and

on
about
the
same
thing.

Even worse, they may demand that we look them in the eyes when *they* are talking.

For an Aspie, that feels like being invaded.

Besides, we usually
listen better
without needing to
work out what all
those facial squints
and twitches mean.

53

Yet, after all our efforts to be helpful and friendly,
we are often excluded or bullied.

Some people may pretend to be our friends,

**while really,
they are not.**

All this makes us sad and
although we might seem calm on the outside...

inside, we are a ball of scream.

The frustrating thing is if people
would simply ask themselves...

I wonder why you
acted that way?

rather than presuming we are bad or stupid,
our lives would be so much easier,

because we always have a logical reason
for what we do, even if we don't know
how to say it in words.

How did I get here?

wire.. balance.. slip..
gravity.. stretch.. ouch

I dunno.

And people who think we don't have emotions are wrong.

Of course we have them, but we aren't always sure which emotions we need to show.

Although our faces may not know the moves,
our hearts do.

Eventually we learn how to act in an acceptable way.

Often, we are good at it.

But that does not mean our Asperger's has disappeared.

It makes us actors who are sometimes
sad and confused on the inside.

After saying all that, we are proud of who we are,
and wouldn't change ourselves even if we could,

because what we
feel, want, believe
and hope for
isn't any different
from anyone else.

We are simply individuals who need our
weaknesses supported, our strengths recognised,
and our abilities encouraged.

So, if people with and without Asperger's
can learn to accept and value each other,
imagine what we can achieve together!